Alkuajatus

Learn to Listen to Yourself 1
ACTIVE BOOK

Combined Internet Service and Book

" Don't give him beliefs or ready answers,
teach him to listen to himself."

Hannu 2013

www.alkuajatus.org

Alkuajatus: Learn to Listen to Yourself 1 Active Book

Copyright: Hannu 2013
Author: Hannu
Cover, illustrations and layout: Hannu
Original language: Finnish
Original title: Opi kuuntelemaan itseäsi 1 aktiivikirja,
            Published 2013, ISBN 9789522866622
Translation: Alkuajatus Translation Team - The responsible translator: Sami
1st edition in English, published 2013

Publisher: Books on Demand GmbH, Helsinki, Finland
Manufacturer: Books on Demand GmbH, Norderstedt, Germany

ISBN: 9789522866929

Table of Contents

Don't copy or plagiarize the thoughts in this book. If you experience them to be worth mentioning, be responsible and tell people about this book, in other words tell them about the source of the thought, not only your own thoughts that are born based on the thoughts in this book. Help people to find the same source. Anything else would be dishonest towards people but also towards yourself.

Alkuajatus is an independent, original thought and an entirety of its own that isn't based on other thoughts. Don't mix different thoughts when you observe matters. Each thought is its own and observes matters from its own viewpoint. They are not the same thoughts, even if they might have similarities or they would consider the same matters.

When we speak of knowledge about our inner world, only the original knowledge has worth. Knowledge of the inside is found only by focusing on the own inside. A study done from the outside doesn't produce knowledge of the inside, it produces knowledge about the reactions and the behavior of the human. That research doesn't have any direct connection to the inside of the human.

Knowledge that is collected on basis of what others have found on the inside is second hand knowledge, and the one telling about it doesn't have a direct connection to the knowledge. Without an own personal observation of the inside it's a product of thinking, a product of the imagination.

The truth is not a cocktail that can be collected here and there according to one's own mind and of seemingly compatible pieces, and it isn't found by studying from the outside and creating it by thinking.

This Work

This work doesn't give you ready answers. This work helps you to observe matters in such way that you find your own answers from your inside.

In this work we focus on the basic matters considering listening to your own self, which are absolutely essential for us to understand if we want to learn to listen to ourselves at all.

Alkuajatus doesn't make anyone to himself. Alkuajatus helps the person to approach his genuine selfhood by observing matters and by insight.

Alkuajatus doesn't tell you how to live, how to be, what is right and wrong, good and bad. All these are questions that each and everyone need to answer to himself.

It's good to focus properly on this book. Without a proper focus it works as well as uneaten food.

It's good to be aware of that no one else can focus on the person's inside besides the person himself. If you won't bother yourself, nothing will change and nothing will get better, but it might get worse.

This book can be focused upon thoroughly and at the same time you can take a step towards greater inner freedom. Or then you can read through it quickly and miss your chance to find what you seek.

The biggest part of what this book gives is born out of the readers own insights, which are the result of good focusing, and those insights are the goal of this book.

Why Bother with Inner Freedom?

We use at least the first two decades of our lives to grow up to be someone else. We have put a lot of effort into it and learned the values and responsibilities the world did teach us.

We might experience that our person is correctly built according to the learned model and we want to reach the promised price, in other words success.

Few want to notice that his person isn't himself and that it doesn't correspond with his own inner will, and that the learned perception of reality isn't true.

 *1. Why do we experience it to be difficult to abandon the learned models?*

Instead, very usually, we want to look for solutions with which we can correct our person in such way that we can be more successful with the fulfilling of the learned dreams.

 *2. Why do we try to correct our person in favor of the learned models?*

We might think that the bad feeling inside us is some kind of flaw that prevents us from fulfilling our will, and we don't notice that the bad feeling is a result of that we are on the wrong path. We are not on our genuine own will's path, but on the path of a will that we have been taught.

The teachings based on the world's thought want us to believe that the inner bad feeling is something that should be corrected so that we could function better according to the taught will.

Focusing on inner freedom solves the problem, the real problem, which is the substitution of our genuine own will with the untrue will that is in accordance with the taught set of values.

Without focusing on inner freedom we can't genuinely be ourselves or be genuinely free. We are prisoners of the learned thoughts, in other words prisoners of the power game's thoughts.

 *3. Why does authenticity require inner freedom?*

Many people can experience that it's heavy to focus on the own inside and that the materialistic goals, which are in accordance with the taught values, and the favor gained by those values are so important that they don't want to abandon them.

It would be good for each and everyone to stop for a moment and ask himself if I want to be my genuine self and fulfill my own will, or do I want to be someone else and a part of the power game and its lie.

 *4. Why doesn't the world's thought, the power game, favor the persons genuine will?*

Someone might experience that the approaching of his real selfhood is heavy and difficult, especially if he needs the outer approval of those who want him to be in accordance with the learned thought and to fulfill their values.

 *5. Is there any effort so great that it would make it unviable to become your own self?*

Thoughts with an outer origin give outer appreciation, and a person that depends on them looks for outer appreciation. He is dependent of the approval and the favor of others. He is a prisoner of outer thoughts and he experiences inner emptiness to the extent he is honest to himself about it.

 *6. Why do the outer valuations make one dependent of outer appreciation?*

Thoughts with their origin in the inner, in other words one's own thoughts, give inner appreciation. The person himself experiences their value and he experiences inner balance. He is not dependent of the appreciation of others. He is inner free and he experiences spiritual satisfaction that comes from the fulfilling of the purpose of his life.

 *7. Why is the appreciation that comes from the genuine own will, the own inner world, not dependent of outer appreciation?*

There is only one true selfhood, one genuine own will.

There are no alternatives, and that fact doesn't change with anyone's opinion, not even one's own.

Therefore one should ask himself that will I focus on inner freedom, or do I continue to abandon myself by being someone else?

How to Focus?

This book can be used in several ways. Regardless of in which way you use it, it's good to notice that the questions are a significant part of the whole, they help you to understand the matter. They strengthen the observation of the matter by putting focus on important things. When your own questions rise up to your mind, focus also on them well and thoroughly.

1. Focus on your own

You can work on your own. Then you focus on the matter in peace and answer the questions by yourself at your own pace.

Answering the questions like this can be good to do by writing them down in a notebook.

It's very essential to focus properly on the matter. The insights don't come as a gift from above. One has to reach them himself.

 *8. Why do one have to work for the insights?*

2. The Insight Evenings

The Insight Evenings are occasions that anyone can arrange at home. Friends gather and enjoy an evening of insights.

Each person needs to have his own book so that the focusing can be as good as possible. It's good to have the book at home as well as on The Insight Evenings.

Each one focuses by himself independently on the chapter.

When everyone is done observing, then all the participants will go through a chosen section together, one chapter at a time. This is done under guidance of the evening's supervisor to make sure that no one has unclear parts in what has been read.

After that the supervisor reads the questions one by one and the participants, of who the supervisor is one, tells about their own insights that were born during or after the reading.

It's good to apply the instructions in The Insight Evening -guide that can be found at the Alkuajatus website on the Activities page. The Insight Evening -guide is free of charge.

It's also good if the supervising person participates in The Insight Mill or Chat, provided by Alkuajatus, but it isn't a must.

The supervisor can change from time to time. The supervisor isn't a teacher, he keeps the discussion on-topic and proceeding with an proper pace. If necessary, he gives out turns of speech.

This form of use usually gives more than focusing by yourself, since you at the same time grow your understanding of how others experience the matter and feel nearness to them. Also, the own insights sharpen when they are spoken of and you may get something from the others that helps you to discover more.

The Insight Evening also builds the group's reality. It's an occasion of good discussion, where each and everyone gets the freedom and space to be open about his thoughts and his view of life.

The Insight Evenings improve the view of life of the participants and the group. The group's improved view of life makes it easier for the participants to improve their view of life even more.

 *9. In what way can The Insight Evening be useful when observing the matter?*

Download the latest version of The Insight Evening -guide on the website www.alkuajatus.org

3. Active Chat on the Internet

The topics of the book are discussed on the Active Chat online.

You can also participate in The Insight Chat and find discussion over some interesting small topics about life.

Check out the website www.alkuajatus.org for the weekly schedule of The Active- and The Insight Chats.

A short instruction for The Insight Evening

The Insight Evening doesn't take away independent work. Notice that independent work is independent observation of the matter. Everyone observes the matter independently and the discussion is to bring forth the very own observations and insights.

To share the insights can help the others and oneself to discover something that otherwise wouldn't have been raised up. It also helps one to see how others understand life and that raises the group's mutual level of understanding.

The purpose is not to ask others what something is or means. Everyone should ask himself that, since only that brings clarity in the matter to oneself. You can listen to others, but you mustn't believe in anything, you have to find the understanding inside you yourself.

 *10. Why is it important that everyone asks himself?*

You mustn't try to shine and make an impression on the others. You have to try to understand and find the insight in the matter for yourself.

The discussion is not a debate, and no one can be demanded to accept any view.

It's good to bring up practical examples from life during the discussion and it's good to remember that the central question is to observe the own person and the own understanding, not to teach or criticize others.

The key to understanding and insight is the responsibility that each person takes of himself and his own understanding. Responsibility in this context is honesty towards yourself.

More detailed instructions are found in the previously mentioned guide.

 *If you want to know more, you can ask questions on the Alkuajatus website www.alkuajatus.org*

How to Observe?

Read this book in peace, don't be hasty. Observe the matters without mixing in your earlier ideas while observing them.

One of the most important things is the way you observe matters and the other things related to the approaching of the matter. Don't underestimate their importance.

Stop at every question to observe them and the answers to them. That helps you to get deeper with your observation.

 *11. Why is it good to observe the questions in peace?*

It's good to read this book several times. Approach the matter each time as it was a new one. Don't hold on to your previously born understanding or try to strengthen it.

When approaching with an open mind every time, you give space for new discoveries, discoveries that otherwise wouldn't have come to mind or would have done so more slowly.

If we hold on to our previous understanding, we are in fact not observing the relation between the written and reality, we are observing the relation between the written and our previous ideas. That doesn't help us to see what the written presents, that limits us within the terms of our previous ideas.

If we are looking for answers that we wish for or answers we think are correct, then we close our eyes from seeing the answers that genuinely come to our mind.

If we are trying to strengthen our previous ideas, then we might be trying to strengthen a thought that keeps us tied to something that isn't of ourselves.

Then we won't notice the answer that we really need and are looking for.

It's good to observe the matter without having an opinion about it, and not to look for certain answers, but instead stay open to what comes into mind.

 *12. Why is an open mind important?*

What to Observe?

This book isn't the actual target of observation, this is a tool for locating and seeing what this book speaks of on the inside. The actual target of observation is the own inside. Then you are observing the inner reality, not outer words.

When you focus several times on the matters this book describes and use it as a help to concentrate, then new insights will rise up into the mind and the understanding of the matter improves.

The outer world and other people can also be observed in the light of Alkuajatus knowledge, but even then it's good to remember to primarily observe the own inside, the own ideas.

 *13. Why is the actual target of observation the own inside?*

You mustn't criticize other persons or the own person, since that isn't to observe the matter, that is to apply some idea.

Then the applied idea is in a viewpoint of the learned thoughts, not in a viewpoint that grows freedom, it suppresses freedom.

Likewise you mustn't criticize the thoughts and answers that rise up to the mind. They are to be observed, not criticized.

 *14. Why mustn't you criticize the thoughts that rise up to the mind?*

The thoughts that rise up to the mind are often like crops that have to grow before it becomes clear what they are. An unhurried and uncompromising observation of the matter makes the crops grow.

What Answers Are We Looking For?

Others opinions or ideas have no worth when we are looking for our own answers.

The own answers don't have to be completely different, but their origin has to be in oneself. Only then does each and everyone understand himself the answers he uses, and they are answers in relation to the own life and the own viewpoint.

They can differ a lot from the common opinion or other people's ideas, and there is no binding outer rule of what the own answers can be or what they should be.

As the only rule can be held that they actually have to be one's own answers to oneself. The more honest one is to oneself, the more genuinely the answers really are one's own.

Then the person himself is answering to himself and that is the only route to own insights in the matter. It's easier to find different outer answers and advice, but only the own ones have worth.

 *15. Why is it important that one himself answers to himself?*

Outer answers have no direct relation to anyone's own genuine will. They are not own answers and the using of them displaces or ignores the genuine own answers, which are the prerequisite for a genuinely independent life. The more central answer regarding life it's a question of, the more important it is to find the own answer.

 *16. How can an outer answer influence the own answer?*

Where Do We Begin?

For us to be able to approach the basic questions of life, we have to begin at the beginning, in other words that we observe how we ended up where we are, in what way and why the learned perception of reality is a lie and also how to approach the truth.

There is reason to observe each matter a lot, several times, so that we can break the dominant position of the learned thoughts when it comes to understanding and defining reality.

 *17. Why does the dominant position of the learned thoughts in the own mind have to be broken?*

We could compare this to that we have walked a stray path very far, a path that the world teaches and promises that it leads to all kinds of good, and also that it's for our own best.

When we have walked that path for some time, we notice that the good and that the for our own best isn't found. Instead we find an empty and meaningless life.

This path is the path of thoughts, a perception of reality that we have followed since we have been taught to follow it.

 *18. Why is disappointment and frustration over life common?*

To find back to the place where the path deviated from our own, we have to walk back the same path.

When we observe thoughts that create our perception of reality and reveal to ourselves what lead us astray, then we are dismantling that path.

With the help of this book we begin the dismantling of the stray path, and as it disappears, we are approaching the path of our genuine own self and our own will, in other words we are approaching inner freedom.

The truth doesn't reward speed or the collecting of knowledge, it rewards solely and exclusively the quality of the understanding of the matter.

In this context quality is nearness to the truth.

19. Why doesn't the truth reward speed or the collecting of knowledge?

How to Reach the Truth?

To reach the truth in the inner world isn't to learn the truth, it's to remember the truth, to bring it back to memory.

Each and everyone has the truth within, it's only hidden underneath the lies.

Therefore thinking doesn't produce results, and the truth can't be found by consequent thinking, and it can't be built based on values that are held as good.

 *20. Why can't the truth be found by thinking?*

Nothing is true because someone has the opinion that it's beautiful and valuable.

That which is true is true, and it doesn't change to please us, and it can't be reached by inventing thoughts that might feel beautiful or that enjoy the acceptance of some people.

The truth is beautiful in itself. The beauty of created thoughts is in the eyes of the beholder.

 *21. Why is the beauty of created thoughts in the eyes of the beholder?*

The way to the truth goes through the revealing of the lies.

When a lie weakens or disappears, then the truth rises up because it has always been there. Without the revealing of the lies the truth can't be found.

 *22. Why does the way to the truth go through the revealing of the lies?*

The finding of the truth and the revealing of the lies is helped by a good and true description of the inner world but only an own personal insight, in other words seeing, takes you there.

 *23. Why does only a personal insight lead to the goal?*

New and More?

It's common for us to want new knowledge and more knowledge.

If this is applied to the observation of the own inner, then the assumption is that the essential thing is the amount of knowledge.

This popular way of thinking is more to look for entertainment than to look for knowledge and it's the archetype of impatience.

 *24. Why does the human want new and more, and doesn't appropriately focus on what is already at hand?*

The understanding of the inner isn't based on the amount of knowledge, it's based on insights of the inner.

The truth, which is what leads to inner freedom, isn't exceedingly much knowledge, first and foremost it's the depth of the insight that opens the truth for the observer.

For us to understand our inner, we have to primarily focus on finding the new in new insights.

It's good to observe new material, but remembering that the observation of the same material repeatedly leads to new insights.

The best insights of the matter begin to come when the topic has been observed until you have gotten tired of it many times. Just when you begin to believe that you won't get anything more out of something, then a new insight is born and it clearly improves the earlier understanding of the matter.

 *25. Why does a patient and repeated observation open up the mind for new insights?*

Don't Believe in Knowledge

There is a seed of lies in belief.

In this context the word belief means that you accept some claim to be true, without finding out if it's true.

If some knowledge is true, it can be observed and questioned a thousand times and it won't fall. The observation strengthens the understanding of the matter, only lies fall because of it.

No knowledge that is true has to be believed in.

Believing will stop the observation of the matter and freeze the person within some thought that he in fact doesn't even have an understanding of, he only accepts it.

The person stops observing reality, he observes the thoughts that are in accordance with his belief.

 *26. Why is there a seed of lies in belief?*

Lies have to be believed in, since they don't withstand observation.

The target of belief can for example be the teachings of some religion, teachings that present themselves as science or moral doctrines without any religious ties.

Any thought that demands a dominant position demands belief.

 *27. Why does the truth withstand observation?*

Can Life and Other People Be Understood?

If we manage to abandon such that isn't true, then we can understand reality such as it is.

When we observe reality, we apply our ideas to explain it. If our understanding is partly or completely lies, then we can't see the reality as it is.

 *28. How do lies influence the ability to see reality?*

The understanding of reality isn't difficult if the mind isn't full of untrue and complicated knowledge.

Lies are usually complicated. Their ability to explain reality in a believable way is based on blurring and covering the truth. They are complicated because their non-functionality is covered up with complicated explanations.

We aren't prevented from understanding life and other people by anything else but the learned ideas, in other words the lies we have been taught and our willingness to hold on to them.

Anything that isn't true is a truth of an imaginary reality, with which we can observe but not actually understand life and other people.

 *29. How does our willingness to hold on to the learned ideas influence our ability to understand life and ourselves?*

To understand someone else isn't unanimity, and not necessarily even acceptance, it's to understand the thought and the reasons.

Can One Heal Oneself?

Yes one can, and no one can do it for someone else.

To heal oneself is to approach the truth, of which follows that the inner clearness grows. It's nothing else.

The reason to the confusion is in the lies that we have learned to hold for truths.

 *30. Why is the reason to the confusion in the lies?*

Confusion is to solve a problem, or to observe life, by applying lies, which means that thoughts are spun around but no real answers are found.

When the person focuses well on knowledge that helps him to find such that is true and he sees the truth with his own eyes, then the influence of the lies weakens and in the end it ceases. That grows the inner clarity and balance.

 *31. Why does the seeing of the truth grow the inner clearness?*

We can find the help to heal that the world's thought offers, but it's not to heal, it's to adapt and to submit to live within the terms of the world's thought, as if it would be the reality that we have to accept since no alternatives exists, or can exist.

The only real healing is the growth of the inner clearness, which is the approaching of the genuine real self, it isn't to submit to anything, or to please some outer idea.

Life Is an Inner Experience

We experience life within ourselves, and we have no other way to experience it.

We might seek and find material pleasures, but the experience is inner even in those cases.

We can seek for pleasure in something that gives outer appreciation, but the experience is inner.

 *32. Why is life an inner experience?*

The only real achievement is the progress and the fulfilling of the genuine own will.

All other achievements are failures, since they lead in the wrong direction and are the fulfilling of a wrong life.

The world's thought guides to a life of outer valuations, where the own inner will is in disfavor since it strives towards a life of own inner valuations, and it can't be lead from the outside.

The genuine own will is in a conflict with the world's thought since its cause is inner freedom, and the inner free doesn't submit to the terms of the power game.

The only way to reach a balanced and unbroken life is to reach inner clarity and with that the genuine selfhood, the own will and the truth.

 *33. Why does only the truth free one to inner clarity?*

The Truth

The truth is ultimately the absolute truth.

The absolute truth is so far away from us, that it's meaningless to ponder or guess over it.

The relevant is to understand the truth on a level that is connected to our genuine own will, since that is the only helpful and useful level of truth for each and every one of us.

The truth has been reached when it has been reached flawlessly on a functional level compared to the need.

 *34. Why do we have to understand the truth on the genuine own will's level?*

To go below it is harmful and to exceed it isn't possible, since it doesn't correspond to our genuine will.

Self doesn't act deviant from its genuine will, even if the person in his imagination believes he would want to.

With the truth we mean the truth about who we are, why we are and how life works.

We have grown up to seek the truth outside of us, since we have grown up to be controlled by outer thoughts.

Even so the truth is within us and it has always been there. We just have to remember it, to restore our connection to it.

 *35. Why might the person strive to deviate from the genuine own will?*

The Lie

Lie is anything that covers the truth.

The world's thought is a lie, since it covers the truth from us.

 *36. Why is the lie anything that covers the truth?*

A lie has no rights, the truth has all rights.

 *37. Why does a lie have no rights?*

A lie is used to create a thought-image that isn't true and in that way influence how someone acts.

Its purpose is to subject and to control others. It's the character of the power game.

The truth rises when lie is revealed and because of that the power game does anything it can to stop the lie from being revealed.

Others can be controlled only by lying.

Without lies there is no power, there is free will.

 *38. Why is there no power without lies?*

The power game offers as a definition of the truth an idea that is within the boundaries of its own perception of reality, and that doesn't reveal the lie of the power game.

The Genuine Selfhood, in Other Words Self

The approaching of the genuine selfhood isn't an intellectual problem, it's an experience problem.

Self isn't within the limited, Self creates the limited.

Thinking and to handle thoughts in a way considered intellectual are all within the limited and they are creations.

 *39. Why isn't the approaching of true selfhood an intellectual problem?*

One can't find oneself by using creations.

Self can't be approached by using thoughts, by creating more thoughts or by developing thoughts. Self creates thoughts from the persons viewpoint, and none of them is Self.

Thoughts are as much Self as the potter is a pot.

 *40. Why can't you find yourself by thinking?*

The approaching of Self is to experience Self in a way where the lie that separates from Self decreases.

 *41. Why does the decreasing of the lies lead to the approaching of Self?*

The Reason of Birth

No one is born to do nothing.

Self doesn't create anything by chance. To come to this world Self needs a reason and it creates that reason itself.

 *42. Why doesn't Self create anything by chance?*

First there is a thought about doing and that is the reason to come to this world, in other words to be born into this world.

This reason is associated with the wholeness that is our mutual original purpose. We don't create separated purposes.

This reason is the own will and that is the only thing why Self creates a person into this world. The own will is a part of the whole and the fulfilling of it is the benefit and will of all own wills.

This reason, the own will, is the persons only obligation in life. All other offered obligations are lies.

 *43. Why is the genuine own will the only obligation that is based on the truth?*

This reason can be fulfilled to the extent the person is inner free.

 *44. How are the genuine own will and inner freedom connected to each other?*

The Person

The person consists of the thoughts that define his reality, and which act as a comparison base while evaluating the outer world.

 *45. Why does the person consist of thoughts?*

Self builds its person starting with the child that is born, and whose mind is empty seen to the life that has just begun.

In life Self uses the person, experiences life from that viewpoint and is as a person limited within that viewpoint, but is as the consciousness still unlimited.

This matter, which is that the mind is empty, doesn't mean that the child would be empty by not being conscious of itself. The child is a self-conscious person from the beginning.

 *46. Why isn't the child unconscious of itself?*

At this point the will created by Self is a will that yet doesn't have a shape, but the child is conscious of it.

Self can't form thoughts into the child's mind according to its will since the child's mind doesn't contain the necessary tools.

Self can create thoughts into the child's mind within the terms of that viewpoint.

 *47. Why can't Self create thoughts based on the genuine own will into the child's mind?*

If the child grows up in an environment that strongly prevents it from forming anything in the true own will's direction, then it's suppressed and grows up to be fully dominated by outer thoughts.

 *48. Why is the child suppressed if the outer help doesn't support the growth of the own original will?*

Self is the one who creates the child's mind, but it's tied to the child's capacity and can only create and act within the limitations of the child's viewpoint, even if Self is unlimited.

We see the person as an actor, but the maker in the background is Self and it can only use the person within the limits of the person.

The person could with good reason be compared to game equipment that Self creates to fulfill its own will.

 *49. Why could the person be compared to game equipment?*

If the person due to outer influence grows up to be something else, then the person isn't within Self's control and it can't be used to fulfill the own will.

 *50. How can outer influence affect the person?*

If the connection to the own will is to some extent preserved in the person, then he can return himself to the true own will's path.

 *51. Why should one return one's own person to the own will's path?*

The Artificial Person

The artificial person is a product of outer learned thoughts.

As a child grows up, he copies his environment and its thoughts.

The child copies a thought. He makes in his mind a thought that corresponds to the offered thought as he understands it.

The child can copy a lot more than the adults want to teach him. He sees more than they are willing to tell him.

He creates the copy himself and places it in his mind. No one else can place anything into his mind, and neither to take anything out of there.

 *52. Why can't anyone else place anything into the person's mind, and also not take anything out of there?*

At start the child copies without questioning, since his person doesn't yet have the abilities to question with.

When the child develops, he can at a growing rate form thoughts himself and therefore also question what he is being taught.

To question the teachings can be very difficult, since the fundamental understanding of life has already been built, and it's no longer within the consciousness in such way that it would be observed, it's being applied.

It already works as the former of the perception of reality and it's the former of ideas while observing, not the object of observation. The person isn't conscious of it as a thought, and can't observe it. It controls the persons' life as a definition of reality.

 *53. Why and how does the fundamental thought, which is in the unconsciousness, influence the person's understanding?*

Our spiritual environment strives to standardize the behavior and thinking in accordance with the world's thought's viewpoint. It wants everyone to define the purpose and reality based on the world's thought, based on outer thoughts.

To grow up into the offered model is an easy alternative, since there is almost no outer resistance to it. If it's fully accepted, then one doesn't experience any conflict with it. People can interact well with each other by behaving and thinking correctly according to that model.

In this way people are easy to control, since an outer thought has been accepted as the dominant and correct thought. People have grown up to ask and use and outer answer to define right, wrong and the purpose.

 *54. In what way has the outer thought been accepted as a dominant factor and why?*

Some people rule and hunger for power, without understanding that an outer thought controls them.

Some have good positions in society and even without knowing it they support the power game, since they are controlled by an outer thought.

Some are at the bottom of the hierarchy, but even they support the power game, since also their thinking is controlled by an outer thought.

They are all a part of the power game, even if in different

viewpoints, and their thoughts and the energy they produce benefits the maintaining of the power game.

 *55. Why and how are all of them supporting the power game, even without knowing it?*

The one who has grown up to be an artificial person is far away from his own original will, since his mind has been filled with untrue thoughts that define the obligations and ties to the environment.

These untrue thoughts are the power game's thoughts, not the person's own.

When the world's thought asks what someone wants, it asks the artificial person, and it doesn't mean the genuine own will, but the artificial will that has been created in accordance with the learned valuations and that chooses the target of its will from the offered suitable alternatives.

And thus is the artificial person born, but he doesn't know that he is an artificial person controlled by an outer thought. He really believes that he is that person. It's his reality.

 *56. Why doesn't he know that he is an artificial person?*

Some people can sense it, some know it, but very few are willing enough to solve this problem.

 *57. Are you willing to solve this problem on your part?*

The Level of Consciousness and Freedom

The person's level of consciousness is the level of finiteness that he is on. It's some distance from the absolute truth.

By definition the level of consciousness fits the original own will, since the own will has been created in accordance with it.

The person's consciousness is dimmed when he adopts the surrounding world's thought, which in our world is a thought that suppresses the inner freedom and is based on the power game.

 *58. Why does the state of the person's consciousness weaken after birth?*

Freedom is the freedom of the starting level of consciousness, and its viewpoint's freedom to be fulfilled.

This freedom is chained by the outer thought that our world teaches and that strives to raise the child to be dominated by it.

It doesn't help one to grow in accordance with the needs of one's own original will. Rather the existence of the own original will is denied or silenced to death.

The problem of inner freedom is the lie of the world's thought. It's the main factor for anything that prevents the inner freedom.

Before this problem has been solved, there is no reason to ponder upon other problems. It's our only problem and the key to freedom.

 *59. Why is the lie of the world's thought, the power game, our only problem?*

Thinking

Thinking is to observe thoughts and to spin them around.

Thoughts are ideas of reality, not reality itself.

If we learn thoughts and think based on them, then we base our thoughts with thoughts, not with reality.

There are numerous teachings that want to place themselves between reality and their observer to tell what something is, and such teaching is to learn ready answers, not to observe reality.

 *60. Why isn't a thought about reality and reality the same thing?*

Alkuajatus isn't the truth, it's a tool to observe the truth. It mustn't be observed as the truth, but to be used as a tool in the observation of the truth.

The descriptions presented by Alkuajatus mustn't be used by trying to think logically and find the truth by thinking.

A person who observes thoughts doesn't observe reality, he observes the thoughts in his mind.

The only way to reach the truth is to observe the truth itself. A thought about it is only an idea about it, it's not the truth.

The truth can't be written or said or drawn as pictures, but it can be described in a way that helps one to approach it.

 *61. Why is the written or any other expression not the truth, but can be a description of the truth?*

The World's Thought

The world's thought is to each person the thoughts that are and are being fulfilled in his living environment.

The world's thought is being fulfilled differently in different cultures and environments, but basically it's the same, only the ways of fulfilling it are different.

The fundamental idea of the world's thought is the power game.

The power game can be a visible strive for power, which shows itself in politics, business and in crime.

It can be the quite invisible maintaining of the power system by accepting the valuations of the power game, and by supporting it with one's work and by exploiting the position it offers.

In any case it expresses itself in all human relations, in the homes as in the schools, in the working life as in the governments.

62. How does the power game show in the human relations in different environments?

The power game is deep in people's minds and it influences the human behavior in the everyday life everywhere and in everything.

All manners, moral, valuations and the perception of reality are built upon it.

63. How does the power game show in the human behavior in different situations?

The power game rewards with power, money and position.

It wants to tie everyone to the power game, because power strives to subject everybody and it also needs losers in the game, since without losers there are no winners, without subjected there are no subjugators, without exploited there is no one who exploits.

It includes winners and losers who are both playing the power game, even if the losers have lost or didn't get the position, money and power. The power game gets its strength from everyone and it shares its strength to its winners.

 *64. How and from where does the power game get its strength?*

The power game is unceasingly preserving and growing power.

The products of the power game are subjecting, wars and crime.

The power game keeps under control all that it can use to strengthen its power, such as the energy, food and resources, and also the land and sea areas. It's everywhere and in everything.

We all take part in it if we accept and submit to it. The artificial person's path is the path of the power game. The power game stands, since we ourselves are unanimous about its maintaining.

A person who begins the path of inner freedom does no longer participate in it, he has begun to break away from it, even if he to some extent still would be attached to it, for example through work and through the learned thoughts or for practical reasons.

 *65. Who are in the power game and support it?*

To submit to the power game is to submit to an outer thought, and the only alternative is inner freedom on the individual level and the free world on the level of mankind.

 *66. Why is the participating in the power game to submit to an outer thought?*

The free world can't be reached with a revolution or in any other way of playing the power game.

As something has been reached, in the same way it will stand, since it's built in accordance with that way, on that principle.

The power game doesn't disappear with power game, with that we can only change the way the power game expresses itself.

 *67. Why can't the free world be reached with a revolution?*

The Free World

The free world is the world of inner freedom, where the persons' lives are lead by their original own will, which is always good.

In that world there are no subjugators, since the own will doesn't subject others, and it doesn't try to boss others, but it respects the right of everyone's inner freedom.

Therefore there isn't any crime, wars or power in that world.

 *68. Why isn't there any crime, wars or power in the free world?*

The society in the free world functions as the sum of free wills, not subjected by some thought.

One who thinks within the power game's terms is of the opinion that such a world is a daydream, a castle in the air that isn't possible.

As a matter of fact, it's fully possible if we understand that the power game exists only because we ourselves are fulfilling it.

Nothing stops us from abolishing it besides the lies that we maintain ourselves.

The power game is based on lies. The free world is based on the truth.

When we stop lying, then we are in the free world.

 *69. How and why can we abolish the power game?*

The Answers

The answer to some question is an answer seen from some viewpoint. That viewpoint is influenced by that period of time, the valuations, the experienced will and our ability to understand reality.

No answer is infinitely the right one, but a fully correct answer seen from some specific viewpoint is the only right answer from precisely that viewpoint.

The world's thought wants us to look for answers in its own viewpoint.

70. Why does the world's thought want us to look for answers in its own viewpoint?

Seen from the viewpoint of our own self we need answers that are answers seen from the viewpoint of our genuine real will.

71. Why do we need answers seen from our own viewpoint?

When we want to know what we want to do, we must first find our genuine real will. To be able to find it, we have to learn to listen to ourselves in a way that is free of outer influence, since otherwise we won't hear ourselves.

72. Why do we have to learn to listen to the genuine self?

The Own Answer

We don't need the ready answers that the environment gladly churns out. We need something that helps us to find our own answers.

The own answer is an exhausting answer to the own question. An answer is exhausting when it's perfect enough at that moment.

The own answer is based on own insight, on the own understanding, and it's an answer to the needs of the true own will. No one can give that answer to you, you have to find it yourself.

A fully own answer is an answer that is right compared to the genuine own will and it's clear to the person himself. The uncertainty attached to the matter ceases. He knows what he wants.

When the own answer is applied in practice, the result is good and seen to life it's functional. The person's life forms in accordance with his genuine will.

 *73. Why is the genuine own answer an important thing?*

The final clarity usually comes step by step. At some point the person experiences to see clearly. With a closer observation he discovers that it wasn't enough and he focuses on the matter again. He raises the quality of the answer.

One should notice that the own answer isn't created by pushing or by being decisive. It's found within, in peace and quiet.

 *74. Why isn't the own answer a product of decisiveness or pushing?*

To Listen to Yourself

To listen to yourself is to listen to the voice of the genuine own inner. The key is honesty towards yourself.

It's not a question about a voice in the sense that the person would hear someone speak, but a feeling that talks to the person.

It's not a product of thoughts and it's in no case a product of the learned acceptable thoughts and ways of thinking.

If the person stops at the commonly accepted values and the commonly defined good and correct answers, then he will never reach his genuine selfhood.

Then he finds the most common way to create a good human. It results in a human that is pretending to be good, which is a human that ingratiates the ideas of the environment.

75. Why will one who is satisfied with the commonly accepted answers never reach his genuine selfhood?

The genuine selfhood and the genuine own will aren't learned, and they aren't defined by the ideas, moral and values that are prevailing in the world, and neither are they defined by the invented needs of society or other people, which all are outer thoughts.

To listen to yourself is to listen to your real selfhood and to find the answers regarding your own life from within. That is original selfhood.

76. What is original selfhood?

How to Go on from Here?

Don't be hasty.

Focus first on this book thoroughly and then move on the next one without haste.

The better you understand the contents of this book, the better you will understand the contents of the next book.

Also go thoroughly trough the chapters that concerns the focusing on matters. They are of great importance and the observation of them will produce insights, even if the reader would experience that he understands them already. It's good to return to them even after you have moved on to the next one.

The better you understand the functionality of the insights, the deeper you can get with the observation of matters.

Depth isn't to shine with thoughts, it's nearness to the truth and there are no shortcuts to it.

If you are of the opinion that this book doesn't give you enough, start reading it from the beginning and focus carefully on the contents of the book. Don't turn the page before you experience to understand the contents of it.

If you don't get anything out of this book, then you won't get anything out of the next book, since the understanding of the next one requires that you understand this one, and not theoretically but by making genuine insights.

Active Chat on the Internet

Each active book has its own Active Chat on the Internet. Participating requires that the participant has this book.

Participation is free of charge to the first owner of this book. The participation of one person is included in the price of this book.

You can find a link to The Active Chat and The Insight Chat on Alkuajatus website, on the front page or in the Activities section.

The Active Chat on the Internet is discussion in Alkuajatus way. You can get a good introductory picture of it in the chapter "How to focus", on page 10 in this book.

On the Activities section on the home page you can find the topical, last version of the Alkuajatus The Insight Mill -guide. It tells how the Active- and Insight Chats work and how you can benefit the most out of them. The guide is free of charge.

Before you participate in The Active Chat, familiarize yourself with The Insight Mill -guide so that you understand it. If you have questions about the chats or The Insight Mill, you can send them from Alkuajatus home page.

If you feel uncertain about writing in the chat, don't feel forced to write anything. Read what the others discuss and when you experience that you are willing to write you own comments, begin to write.

You can be unknown, anonymous, in the chats if you want.

You can also participate in The Insight Chats with interesting small topics about life.

www.alkuajatus.org

Hannu:
Alkuajatus
The Original Thought
The Little Manual of Life

This book presents the basics of Alkuajatus and with its help you can deepen your view. Read more on the website.

Paperback, 15,5 x 22 cm, 280 pages - ISBN 9789522865304

Hannu:
Learn to Listen to Yourself 2 Active Book

The second part in the Learn to listen yourself series. How do we find ourselves and how can we reduce the outer influence. The book will be found on the website when published.

To be published 2013

Hannu:
Broken Heart's Active Book

Focus on the problem of broken hearts in a way that helps you find understanding of the real reasons, and grow your inner freedom regarding the so called matters of the heart. A good book for love matters, even if the heart isn't broken.

To be published 2013

www.alkuajatus.org

Sign up in the email list at the home page and receive information about Alkuajatus happenings directly in your email.

Give yourself a chance, focus thoroughly in the most central matter of your life, in other words your genuine own will.

The world teaches you how to find material items and the artificial person. Alkuajatus teaches you how you find yourself and a genuinely own life.

www.alkuajatus.org